ACT UPON A STORY

A Series of Skits about Joseph

by Guy & Teresa Lavergne

About the authors:

Guy and Teresa Lavergne worked with children for over 35 years.

They were part of a church ministry staff for 21 years.

During that time, they wrote skits for children, which were performed by children, teens, or adults for the children's worship services, chapel services, and special events.

Their first published book, Act Upon a Story: 60 Bible Skits for Ministry, contained skits written for children. There is a skit for almost all of the major Bible characters.

In reviewing that book for publication, they realized that one major Bible character had been left out. There were no skits about the eleventh son of the patriarch Jacob of the Old Testament. The story of Joseph could not be adequately told in one skit, so they decided to make a sequel to the first book, which would be solely about Joseph. The skits in this edition are more appropriate for older children, youth, and adults. They could be used in a variety of ways; as introductions for a series of messages, or combined into one longer presentation or combined into several longer skits.

Joseph's life story continues to impact and teach and inspire people, because of his trust in God. It is the heartfelt desire of the authors that audiences will perceive the hand of God at work in the events of their own lives, as the story of Joseph comes to life on the stage.

CONTENTS

PART 1:   THE COLORFUL COAT

You will need a divider or curtain. We often used part of a portable puppet stage.

Two of Joseph's brothers enter and go behind the curtain. Joseph enters and goes to stand in front of the curtain, and appears to be waiting for something. He hears a noise and puts his ear to the curtain. The brothers suddenly come from behind the curtain and see him.

Simeon: *(accusing, threatening tone of voice)*   **What are you doing?**

Levi: *(angry, insolent tone of voice)*   **Are you spying on us again?**

Joseph: *(matter of fact)*   **Father told me to wait for him here.**

Simeon: *(contemptuous)*   **Daddy's little favorite.**

Levi: *(mocking)*   **You always do just what Father wants, don't you.**

Joseph: *(earnestly)*   **I thought that's what I am supposed to do.**

Simeon: *(malicious)*   **We know your true motives, you little phony.**

Levi: *(vehement)*   **You're playing up to Father so you can steal our inheritance!**

Simeon: *(He notices someone approaching)*   **Father's coming! We can't let him see us here.**

Levi: *(to Joseph)*   **If you say anything about us to him, you're dead.**

Simeon and Levi quickly hide behind the curtain. Jacob arrives and goes up to Joseph.

Jacob: *(affectionately)*   **Joseph, my son. You did just as I asked.**

Joseph: **Yes, Father.**

Jacob: **I have a gift for you, for your seventeenth birthday.**

Jacob holds up a robe he had hidden inside his own robe.

Joseph: *(He is surprised and very happy)* **Thank you, Father.**

Jacob stands behind Joseph, and lovingly assists him in putting it on.

Jacob: **For you, my son. When you wear this, remember how deeply I love you.**

Joseph: **I will, Father. I am very grateful.** *(he embraces his father)*

Jacob: *(soberly)* **I must ask you something.**

Joseph: **Yes, Father?**

Jacob: **Have you seen your brothers, Levi and Simeon?**

Joseph: *(hesitantly)* **Yes, Father.**

Jacob: **Can you tell me where they are? They are not with the flock of sheep.**

Joseph: *(pause to show reluctance)* **They are behind this curtain.**

(Simeon and Levi come out and face their father with a sullen defiant attitude)

Jacob: **What is the meaning of this? Who is guarding the sheep?**

Simeon: *(disdainful)* **Don't worry, Father. Nothing's going to happen to the sheep.**

Levi: *(defensively)* **We just needed a little break, that's all.**

Jacob: *(sternly)* **Go back immediately and do your duty! Joseph, you and I shall talk more a little later. I must see about your other brothers.** *(he exits)*

Simeon: *(to Joseph)* **You just couldn't keep your big mouth shut, could you!**

Joseph: **I could not lie to Father.**

Levi: You little angel! Don't pretend with us---we know what you're <u>really</u> like.

Simeon: Well, well, well....look at this. A coat of many colors, a symbol of honor.

Levi: Father never gave us one of those.

Simeon: I guess we're just not special enough. Who do you think you are, anyway?

Joseph: Your brother.

Levi: Half-brother. <u>Only half.</u> Don't forget that.

Joseph: We have the same father....

Simeon: Oh, yes, your poor barren mother finally had <u>you</u>. And that makes you SO special.

Levi: Tell me, who did God bless the most? Your mother...or our mother who was able to have many children?

Joseph: I can't say; I don't know all of God's plans.

Simeon: Well, keep your mouth shut from now on, and don't tell Father our business.

Levi: *(mocking)*   Oh, and try to keep that nice new robe clean!

Joseph watches sadly as his brothers walk away.

PART 2: THE DREAMS BEGIN

Joseph's older brothers are seen together in one place, in small groups of 2 or 3.

Simeon: Did you hear about Joseph's latest dream?

Levi: He had another one? The first one was bad enough---all our sheaves of wheat bowing down to his. *(disgusted)*

Simeon: This one even annoyed Father. He said he saw the sun, the moon and eleven stars bowing down to him.

Levi: I take it that the stars represent us----his eleven brothers.

Simeon: Something must be done to stop him.

Levi: It's only a dream; what can he do with that?

Simeon: Use it to convince Father that he has the divine right to rule our family.

Slight pause as Levi looks outward and notices something of intense interest.

Levi: Well, well, well! Look who is coming now...this just might be our chance.

Reuben: *(he has joined their group)* Chance for what?

Simeon: To get rid of this dreamer.

Reuben: *(incredulously)* Are you speaking of murder?

Levi: Have you got a better plan to permanently be free of him?

Reuben: He is our brother!

Simeon: *(scornfully)* Half-brother.

Reuben: Even so, let us not be guilty of murder! I saw a deep hole not far from here; we can leave him in there and let a wild animal kill him.

Joseph arrives and comes to meet his brothers, who by now are all in one group.

Levi: *(phony)* **Welcome, little brother! What a pleasant surprise to have you visit us.**

Joseph: **Father sent me to see how you are doing.**

Simeon: **Oh, ho! Father's little helper has come to check on his big brothers.**

Levi: **You won't be giving a bad report this time, you little jerk.**

Levi, Simeon, and 2 others grab him and hold him.

Simeon: *(he stands back to view the captive)* **Take that coat off of him.**

The brothers holding him comply and viciously pull it off.

Joseph: *(shocked)*   **What are you doing? ----- my brothers!**

Simeon: **Only what we have wanted to do for a long time. Where's the hole, Reuben?**

Reuben: **Follow me.**

Have some kind of barrier, stage set prop, or curtain set up to hide the area of the "hole".

Joseph's brothers herd him towards the hole, led by Reuben.

Joseph: **No!!! Please don't do this!!**

Use sound effects to simulate the brothers throwing him down into the pit.

Levi: **What will become of your dreams now, little brother!**

Joseph: *(muffled voice, sounding far away)* **I beg of you, don't do this!**

Simeon: **Let's go have some lunch.**

> *The brothers begin to walk away.*

Joseph: **Help, somebody help me!!**

Simeon: **No one cares, so just shut up!** *(he yells in Joseph's direction as they walk away)*

> *The brothers exit defiantly.*

Narrator: But of course, there <u>was</u> someone who heard his cry for help---someone who cared very much.

Joseph: **Oh, God, I know you have not forgotten me.....please be with me.... and protect me.**

Narrator: And that is exactly what God did, as we shall see.

PART THREE: SOLD INTO SLAVERY

Joseph is in the "pit" while his brothers walk in and stand nearby talking together.

Narrator: Joseph, the young Hebrew boy, began having strange dreams that made him look as if he were destined to rule over his brothers.   After he told his family about these dreams, his brothers began to hate him so much that they wanted to get rid of him.   They would have killed him, but Reuben the oldest brother, prevented this, and convinced them to throw Joseph into a deep hole instead. Joseph is there now, at the bottom of an empty well.

Judah: <u>Now</u> what do we do?

Levi: Nothing. He's not our problem anymore.

Simeon: I'm sure not going to stand around all day waiting to see if an animal kills him.

Reuben: *(Reuben is uneasy and paces)* **I need to run an errand. I will be back very soon. Don't do anything foolish while I am gone.** *(he exits)*

Simeon: What's bothering him?

Levi: Only that he stands to lose the most if Father finds out what we did.

Simeon: Like, Father might write him out of the will and he would lose his inheritance?

Levi: Exactly. He went soft on the boy and wouldn't kill him. I bet he has plans to get him out of the pit, too.

Judah: Reuben wants to look like the hero to Father, so I bet he's going to try to rescue Joseph. Then all the rest of us will look bad to Father.

Simeon: What do you suggest?

Judah: Look, there's the answer!

(he points in the direction of some slave traders coming)

Simeon: Slave traders! We can actually make some money out of this deal.

Levi: He's young, and handsome---we can get a good price for him.

Along with 2 other brothers, they haul Joseph out of the pit, and hail the slave traders. The slave traders approach and prepare to bargain for Joseph.

Simeon: We've got something you might be interested in!

Trader: Some thing or someone?

Levi: This strong young man---he's smart, educated, good-looking...

Trader: Can he work?

Simeon: Like a mule.

Trader: *He feels Joseph's muscles and examines his teeth.*

Levi: I think he'll fetch a good price at the market.

Trader: You think so? Okay, I will give you 10 pieces of silver.

Simeon: He's worth 30.

Trader: No. We will be on our way.

Levi: We can't let him go for less than 25.

Trader: I will give you 20. That is all.

Simeon: Agreed.

Joseph: Brothers! I plead with you---do not do this---our father will die from grief!

Trader:	**Sold!** (*he hands Levi the money bag*) **Now we must be on our way.**

The slave traders tie Joseph's hands and push him to make him get in line as they exit.

Levi:	(*He opens the bag and looks in*) **Twenty pieces of silver----not bad. I think we got a good deal.**
Joseph:	**My brothers! Help me!!**
Trader:	(*he threatens Joseph*) **Silence!! Your brothers do not care.**

The slave traders exit with Joseph walking in between them.

(Reuben comes back just in time to see Joseph vanishing with the slave traders)

Reuben:	**What have you done! I told you not to do anything foolish!**
Levi:	(*matter-of-fact*) **We didn't. We actually made a profit.**

(Levi shows Reuben the money bag)

Reuben:	**Profit! You think we will profit from this? And how do you think we will explain this to Father? And if he ever finds out the truth....** (*anguished*)
Simeon:	(*flippantly*) **I didn't know you cared this much.**
Reuben:	**I care about our Father.**
Judah:	**Look here, I have an idea. We've got his robe. We'll put the blood from a goat on his robe and show it to Father. He will think a wild animal killed him.**
Levi:	**Good thinking, Judah! You have just solved a huge problem for all of us.**

Reuben: (bitterly) Oh, yes…that part. But how do you expect to comfort Father in his grief? He loved Joseph more than any of us, and you know it!

Simeon: (sarcastically) I think we're well aware of that by now. But we're free now from that troublemaker and his dreams!

Reuben: (grimly) No, we are not. We will carry this guilt for the rest of our lives.

The brothers soberly pack up and exit.

PART 4---POTIPHAR'S HOUSE

SLIDE: Show a scene representing ancient Egypt as the background setting.

Narrator: Joseph had ten older brothers who were extremely jealous of him. When he began having dreams that made him look more important than his brothers, they were infuriated. They planned to get rid of him. Reuben the oldest brother was more protective than the others, and tried to keep them from harming Joseph. But while Reuben was away, the other brothers sold Joseph to a band of travelling slave traders. These traders carried Joseph away to the land of Egypt, and took him to the slave market to sell him as a slave.

The slave traders enter from the back, and march Joseph up to the front.
(Remember to leave a central area to be designated as the home of Potiphar.)
Potiphar enters from the side accompanied by a guard, and approaches the traders.

Potiphar: **I am looking for another household servant.**

Trader: **How about this one? He's strong!** *(In a rough whisper to Joseph: "**Stand up straight!**")*

Potiphar: **How old is he?**

Joseph: **I am seventeen, sir.**

Potiphar: *(He starts to walk away)* **That may be a bit too young.**

Trader: **Oh, but he is smart....and very healthy!** *(In a rough whisper, he commands Joseph: "**Show your teeth!**")*

Potiphar: **How much do you want for him?**

Trader: *(sly)* **Forty pieces of silver will be a bargain for a fine slave like this...**

Potiphar: **I think it's rather high. I will give you thirty.**

11

Trader: Oh, but that is what I had to pay for him! I am just a poor man with many mouths to feed....no, no, I cannot accept thirty.

Joseph: He paid twenty pieces.

Trader: *(he threatens Joseph: "shut up!")* A slight mistake, sir....I remember now---it was twenty.

Potiphar: Then I will give you thirty.

Trader: Very good. He is yours, Captain Potiphar. *(he eagerly takes the money, then exits)*

Potiphar's guard takes the rope attached to Joseph's hands and leads him to Potiphar's "house". Have a small curtain divider set up (such as part of a puppet stage) in one side of the "house".

While the narrator reads, have the actors "mime" (silent acting) Potiphar giving instructions to Joseph. Joseph can act out several chores, such as cleaning the floor, bringing water, serving food or drink to Potiphar, fanning him with a large palm leaf "fan", writing on a tablet as if receiving instructions, etc.

Narrator: Joseph was now separated from his family and all that was familiar, by hundreds of miles. He was no longer the favorite son; he was living the life of a slave in a foreign country. He had no friends in this strange place. And yet he knew that he was not alone---he knew that the Lord was with him. And after a while, Potiphar realized this too, because the Lord blessed Potiphar's household for Joseph's sake. The Lord blessed Joseph's abilities also. Joseph became so skilled that Potiphar asked him to manage everything he owned. Potiphar trusted Joseph completely. Joseph missed his homeland, but he did his best at all his work, in order to honor the Lord. Despite all that, there was trouble coming.

Potiphar's wife comes out from behind the small curtain. She & Joseph are alone.

She slyly exhibits a provocative seductive manner.

P's wife:	*(sultry)* Hello, Joseph. You have become such a fine young man — I have something I want to give you. You can come to my room; it's private.
Joseph:	I know what you want, and it's wrong. You belong to another, and I will not touch you.
P's wife:	No one will know about this but you and me.
Joseph:	My God sees everything that we do. He has been with me since my youth; how could I go against His commands and dishonor Him? My master trusts me with everything in his house; how could I betray him like this?
P's wife:	*(angrily she grabs him by the arm)* So you refuse me? You despise me?

Joseph jerks away from her, and his "jacket" comes off. He leaves it and runs out.

P's wife:	*(very loudly)* Guards!!!!! Go after the slave!

Two guards rush out and apprehend Joseph and bring him back. Potiphar comes in.

Potiphar:	What is the meaning of this?
P's wife:	It seems the authority you gave this slave has gone to his head. He thinks he can have anything he wants----including your wife.
Potiphar:	What?
P's wife:	He attacked me, and would have violated me, but I screamed and he ran. I have his coat as proof of this.
Joseph:	Master, I have not betrayed you.
Potiphar:	You dare to call my wife a liar? If I were not merciful, I would have you executed this moment! But I never want to see your face again.

Potiphar: Guards, you will take him to prison.

(Potiphar stalks out and the guards prepare to take Joseph away)

P's wife: **Just a moment.** *(she looks scornfully at Joseph)* **You will never be anything more than a slave....and now you will rot in prison.**

She exits haughtily and the guards take Joseph away.

Narrator: And so Joseph was taken away to prison, although he had done nothing wrong. Yet the Lord was still with him, even in that dark place, as we shall see.

PART FIVE---PRISON LIFE

NARRATOR: Joseph was just a teenager when he was sold as a slave and taken to the land of Egypt. A prominent wealthy man named Potiphar bought Joseph to be a household servant. Joseph trusted in the Lord, and became very successful at whatever he did. When Potiphar saw Joseph's abilities as a manager, and the way God blessed Joseph's work, he put Joseph in charge of everything he owned. Potiphar's wife was secretly attracted to Joseph and wanted him to be her lover. When Joseph refused, she lied about him, and Joseph was sent to prison.

Joseph is roughly escorted into the prison room by a guard. The guard exits.
Two other prisoners occupy the room and are sitting on a bench or the floor.
The warden enters with a book and pen and questions Joseph in a terse manner.

Warden: Name?

Joseph: Joseph, sir.

Warden: Occupation?

Joseph: I was a slave in Potiphar's household.

Warden: Nationality?

Joseph: I am a Hebrew, sir.

Warden: Let's get one thing straight: we don't like your kind around here. You break a rule, you're dead.

Joseph: I understand, sir.

Warden: Good.   *(He goes to sit down at a table a little distance away.)*

Prisoner 1:   So what did you do to end up in prison? Steal something?

Prisoner 2:   Are you a run-away slave?

Joseph: No. I refused to do something wrong, and it made someone angry.

Prisoner 1:   Ha! That's a laugh. *(sarcastically)* We're in here because we <u>did</u> something wrong, and you're in here because you wouldn't.

Joseph: (calmly) Potiphar didn't think the lie this person told was very funny, and so here I am.

Prisoner 2:   Hmmm....tough luck. *(somewhat sympathetically)*

Just then the warden makes an exasperated sound and bangs his fist on the table.

Joseph: Is there anything I can do to help you?

Warden: *(he looks up, surprised)* What? Are you educated?

Joseph: Yes; I was Potiphar's household manager over all his supplies and property.

Warden: *(he walks over to Joseph and shows him the book)* These figures are not coming out right. See if you can find the mistake.

Joseph: *(he looks carefully at the book for a few seconds)* It's right here, sir.

The warden looks astonished, takes the book, and goes back to his desk, looking amazed. Then he beckons to Joseph, who gets up and follows him to another "room".

Narrator: There were many more occasions like that in which the warden found Joseph to be so helpful and responsible, that eventually, Joseph became the manager of the prison. His kindness and genuine concern for people and his hope in God caused others to trust him. When the king became angry with two of his servants, and threw them into prison, it was Joseph who looked after them and gave them encouragement to endure prison life. One morning, he noticed that the new prisoners looked very disturbed.

This occurs during the above narration: Two guards escort the new prisoners into the jail. Joseph comes back in and meets them cordially (in a friendly manner), then he exits again.

Joseph: *(he comes back in and notices how sad the butler and baker look)* **You both look so troubled. Tell me what is wrong; maybe I can help.**

Butler: **It's these dreams....we both had very strange dreams, and we can't figure out what they mean.**

Joseph: **The God I serve can explain dreams; tell me your dreams.**

(If you have visuals of the dreams to put on a large screen, it would enhance this scene.)

Butler: **I was the royal cupbearer for the king. It was my duty to bring Pharaoh, king of Egypt, his cup of wine---and to make sure that no one had poisoned it. In my dream, I saw a vine with three branches. These began to make buds, which immediately blossomed, and then immediately became clusters of ripe grapes. In my dream, I took a handful of grapes and squeezed them into Pharaoh's cup---and then I put the cup into Pharaoh's hand.**

Joseph: **This is the meaning of your dream: the three vines are three days. Within 3 days, the king will have you restored to your former position as his cupbearer.**

Butler: **Who <u>are</u> you? And where did you get such wisdom?**

Joseph: **I am a descendant of Abraham, and I serve the one true God who created everything. Wisdom comes from knowing Him. When you are restored, please tell Pharaoh about me---for I have done nothing to deserve being in prison.**

Baker: **My dream is similar. There were three baskets of bread on my head. The top basket was full of baked goods, and there were birds eating out of the basket.**

Joseph: *(sighs)* **This is the meaning of your dream: Within 3 days, the Pharaoh will have you hanged, and the birds will eat your flesh.**

Baker: *(angrily)* **What kind of God do you serve!----that would allow his servant to rot in prison, and would give me hope only to send me to my death?!**

Joseph: **I do not understand all of His ways, but I trust Him. I know that He cares about all people, and He has given you a dream to warn you so that you could be prepared.**

Baker: *(bitterly)* **And how does a person prepare to die? What would you know about that?**

Joseph: **I have come close to death. And I can tell you that knowing God is the only way to take away the fear of death. But to know Him, you must first trust Him.**

Baker: **Tell me about this God of yours.**

Joseph, the baker, and the butler continue to mime having a conversation.

Narrator: So Joseph did, and it was a timely revelation, for just as Joseph had predicted, within three days Pharaoh had the baker executed. And Pharaoh also restored the royal cupbearer to his former station.

The executioner comes to the prison and escorts the baker away, after Joseph embraces him. Then a guard comes to take the butler back to the palace, and Joseph bids him farewell.

Joseph: **Goodbye, my friend. I am very glad for you. When all is well with you, remember me----and tell them of my case.**

Butler: **How could I ever forget you!** *(He exits with the guard)*

Narrator: But he did forget. In fact, two full years went by before he even thought of Joseph again. But time in Heaven is not the same as it is here on earth; the Lord had not forgotten Joseph. The time had not yet come when God's secret plan would be revealed.

PART SIX---AT THE PALACE

NARRATOR: the young Hebrew man named Joseph had certainly experienced some negative circumstances in his life. He was sold into a life of slavery by his own brothers, and brought to a foreign country by the slave traders. He had no friends or family here, but the Lord's presence was with him, and he chose to honor God in every situation. When he was falsely accused and thrown into prison, he refused to spend his time in depression and doubt. Instead he trusted God for the outcome, and did everything he could to help other people. Years went by as he waited...and then suddenly----God opened a new door into the place where Joseph's dreams became a reality.

Joseph is seated on a bench at a rough table. He is doing bookwork for the warden of the jail. The warden comes hurriedly into the prison with a very excited nervous manner.

(You will need a free-standing room screen or divider for this scene, and some sort of Egyptian tunic which can be pulled easily over a shorter tunic.)

Warden: **Joseph, go change clothes. Here, put this on. You need to be presentable.**

Joseph: **Yes, sir.** *(He goes behind the screen and pulls the tunic over his prison garb. He asks questions as he dresses)* **Can you tell me what this is about, sir?**

Warden: **Pharaoh has summoned you to the palace!**

Joseph: **Is this a pardon?.......or a trial?....am I to be executed?**

Warden: **No, none of that!   Pharaoh has had a dream!**

Joseph: *(Joseph steps out from behind the screen)* **A dream? How did he know about me?**

Warden: **The butler! Do you remember him?**

Joseph: Yes, the Lord gave me the meaning of his dream. I remember him, but it seems he did not remember me.

Warden: He didn't----until the king had two strange dreams that no one could make any sense out of.

Joseph: So I am going into the courtroom of Pharaoh, king of Egypt.

Warden: May your God be with you. This could be dangerous....especially since he did not sleep well on account of these troubling dreams, and his counselors failed to give him an explanation.

Joseph: Do not worry. No matter what happens, the Lord is in charge of my life. He is always faithful, and we can trust him.

Warden: It's Pharaoh I don't trust. Be careful what you say.

Joseph: The Lord will give me the words to say.

Pharaoh's guard comes to escort Joseph to the palace. They exit.

Remove the screen, and bring in a throne.

Pharaoh enters and sits on his throne, with advisors standing by him.
Joseph enters, escorted by the guard. He approaches Pharaoh and kneels.

***Make sure that the throne is at an angle to the audience, so that Joseph's profile is seen as he talks. (and so that his back is not facing the audience)

Pharaoh: You may stand. So you are Joseph, the Hebrew.

Joseph: *(stands)* Yes, sir, I am.

Pharaoh: And how is it that you have the power to explain the meaning of dreams, when my advisors could not?

Joseph: I do not have this power, sir. It is God who gives the meaning of dreams.

Pharaoh: We have many gods in Egypt. And yet it seems that not one of them has this power. I do not know your God, but I will be very interested to hear what He has to say.

Joseph: He will not withhold the meaning from you; that I am sure of.

Pharaoh: This is what I dreamed: I was standing by the river, and I saw 7 fat cows come out of the river, and graze by its banks. Then 7 gaunt, emaciated cows came out of the river, and they ate up the 7 fat cows. But afterwards the 7 thin cows looked just as bony and scrawny as before. In my second dream, I saw 7 heads of wheat on a stalk, and they were very ripe and plump and golden. Then another stalk of wheat grew up, but the heads on it were withered and shriveled and black. Then the dark wheat swallowed up the golden ones.

Joseph: The two dreams have the same meaning. God has shown Pharaoh what He is about to do. Since God has given two dreams, it means that this event will most certainly happen, and nothing can stop it. But God in His mercy has given you warning so that you may be prepared.

Pharaoh: *(leaning forward anxiously)* **What is it? What is going to happen?**

Joseph: The seven fat cows and the seven healthy grains of wheat mean that there will be seven good years of abundant food in Egypt, and after that will come seven years of famine. During the 7 good years, you must prepare for the bad ones, or people will starve. The famine will be severe and it will affect all of Egypt.

Pharaoh: How could we prepare for such a disaster?

          Pharaoh looks around at his advisors, but none of them has any ideas.

Pharaoh: *(to Joseph)* **Do you have a suggestion?**

Joseph: Yes…Pharaoh should choose a capable man of integrity and put him in charge of this project. Pharaoh should appoint a steward over each area in Egypt to collect 1/5 of the harvested crops during the plentiful years. These stewards will reserve the food in special storehouses, under the authority of Pharaoh.

Pharaoh: I shall discuss this plan with my advisors.

Joseph: Yes sir.

Joseph steps to the side as the advisors gather around Pharaoh and pretend to discuss the matter. The advisors all nod their heads in approval, and step back away from Pharaoh. Pharaoh motions to Joseph, and Joseph approaches again. (Remember to have Joseph positioned so that the audience sees his profile)

Pharaoh: We have agreed on this plan, and also that we could not find a person more suited to supervise this project than this man Joseph, who has the Spirit of God residing in him.

Joseph: *(bowing slightly in deference)* I am at your service.

Pharaoh: Your God has obviously chosen you because He revealed the meaning of the dreams to you. You did not take the credit for this wisdom, and therefore I know that I can trust you and put you in charge of my palace and my people.

Joseph: I will do my best, with God's help.

Pharaoh: And because you rely on your God's strength and guidance, I will put you in charge of the entire land of Egypt. Your authority will be the greatest in the land, after mine.

During the following narration, these things are acted out silently: Pharaoh summons an attendant to bring Joseph a very fine "coat" and the attendant puts it on Joseph; then the attendant puts a gold chain around Joseph's neck; then Pharaoh shows Joseph a signet ring and mimes speaking to Joseph about the significance of the ring, and Pharaoh puts it on Joseph's finger. Joseph bows slightly, and then Pharaoh exits, followed by the others.

Narrator: In one day, Joseph went from being a slave in prison, to second in command in the most powerful nation in the world at that time. Did this make Joseph proud? No, all of his suffering before this had prepared him to take this responsibility in the most mature way---in a humble way. He had learned to rely on God and trust in Him, and nothing could shake that trust now.

PART SEVEN: RULING IN EGYPT

NARRATOR: If anyone had reason to call himself a victim of negative circumstances, it would be Joseph. He was sold by his family members into slavery at the age of seventeen; he was thrown into prison for a crime that he did not commit, and he was forgotten by people he had helped. In the natural state of things, it would be very reasonable for a person in his situation to become bitter and angry, depressed and full of self-pity. But Joseph had learned to live in the supernatural---he lived by faith in God and not by what he saw around him. He knew that what is visible is temporary, and what is invisible is far more important. Finding favor with God through faith became Joseph's priority for life. And God rewarded him openly, as we shall see.

Pharaoh and Joseph enter, talking as equals;
they stop center front stage for this conversation.

Pharaoh: I know that you are a Hebrew----and that is inconsequential to me because of the divine favor you possess----but still I think you should have an Egyptian name since you represent me. This name will be your title.

Joseph: Whatever you choose, sir, I will be grateful.

Pharaoh: I shall call you Zaphenath-Paneah, which means revealer of secrets and savior of the land.

Joseph: I am honored, sir, by your choice.

Pharaoh: Your God has sent you here to rescue our people from starvation, and so I am grateful to your God and I will take care of His servant.

Joseph: I am ready to begin my duties.

Pharaoh: Very well. My attendants will ready my royal chariot. You must take a tour of Egypt in my chariot, so that all will know you have my authority.

Joseph: Yes, sir. I will prepare to leave. *(Joseph bows and begins to walk away)*

Pharaoh: Just a moment, Joseph---there is one more thing we must do before you leave.

Joseph walks back to the Pharaoh.

Pharaoh: There are some who may have trouble accepting a Hebrew shepherd as a ruler. Yet if you marry into the family of the royal priests, they cannot question your position. You will truly be Egyptian.

Joseph: I respect your wisdom. Is there someone you have in mind?

Pharaoh: Yes; she is Asenath, daughter of Potiphera, priest of On. I have already spoken with her father, and made the arrangements. I think she will please you well.

Pharaoh exits, and Asenath comes in escorted by an attendant, and goes up to Joseph. Joseph is very stunned by her beauty, and graciously takes her hand and speaks (mimes) earnestly to her. They quietly exit, miming a conversation, followed by the attendant.

Narrator: And here we shall respect their privacy as Joseph becomes acquainted with his bride. Joseph was thirty years old when he began his service to Pharaoh, and he traveled all over Egypt, collecting 1/5 of all crops and putting this surplus away in storehouses. All went well during the seven years of plenty, and two sons were born to Joseph and Asenath.

Joseph and Asenath come out, accompanied by their two sons, who begin to play with some toys, while Joseph and Asenath sit and watch them.

Asenath: Manasseh looks so much like you. And does he truly make you forget your past and all the pain you suffered at the hands of your brothers?

Joseph: He does. And when I look at Ephraim, I know that God has made me fruitful---He has given me hope in the land of my suffering.

Asenath: And when I look at you, I do not see a shepherd, I see a Prince with God. I am continually amazed that you never took on the mentality of a slave.

Joseph: I knew that God is with me; His presence kept me from that.

Asenath: My father taught me to worship the sun, but you have taught me to worship the One who made the sun.

Joseph: *(smiles at the memory)* My father taught me to love God, when I was their age. *(indicating his boys)* I only wish I knew if he were still alive.

Just then, a messenger arrives to speak with Joseph. He is anxious and upset.
(One of Joseph's attendants comes into the room with him.)

Messenger: Forgive my intrusion my lord, but I felt you would need this information immediately. We have word from the most distant province that the famine has begun.

Joseph: *(to his attendant)* Prepare my chariot. I must leave immediately.

Asenath: *(to the boys)* Come, children. *(they go to her)* Your father must go on a journey. We will help him get ready.

Joseph: *(He hugs the boys)* Do not be afraid. God will take care of us.

Joseph exits with Asenath and the boys, and the attendant exits with the messenger.

Narrator: And that became the primary message of Joseph's life: that God will take care of us. His presence is real; even more real than the physical objects around us. And it is in His presence that we experience real life.

PART EIGHT: THE TEST BEGINS

Narrator: The fate and survival of an entire nation now rested on the shoulders of a young Hebrew man, who had once been a slave and a prisoner. It was during those times in his life, that God prepared him for such a great responsibility. The famine spread quickly over the land of Egypt, and became very severe as God had revealed it would to Joseph through Pharaoh's dreams. As people began to run out of food, they came to Joseph to buy grain. Egypt was not the only country to experience famine. The entire world was affected by the famine, and people from other countries also came to Egypt to buy grain from Joseph.

While the narrator is saying the lines above, Joseph comes out and sits on a raised platform while Egyptians come to speak to him. The attendants usher people in and out of Joseph's reception area. Then Joseph's brothers are seen entering from the back of the room, and Joseph sees them.

Steward: My Lord? You look pale; are you ill?

Joseph: Those men who just came in are my brothers.

Steward: What should I do?

Joseph: Do not let them know who I really am. I will have to pretend that I don't know the Hebrew language; I will need you to translate for me.

Steward: Yes, my lord. I will do this. Is there anything else?

Joseph: Yes, I need you to detain them for a moment, so that I can be alone to pray.

Steward: It shall be done.

Joseph exits, while the steward goes up to Joseph's brothers, and escorts them off stage.

Narrator: Joseph needed to find out what kind of men his brothers had become, in his absence. He decided to give them a test of character, before he would reveal his identity. If he would dare to trust his brothers again, he would first have to know if their hearts were still ruled by jealousy.

Joseph enters again, and goes to sit on the raised platform. The steward enters, escorting Joseph's brothers to a place which is some distance from the platform. The steward remains standing beside the platform. Joseph quietly tells him what to say to his brothers, and he conveys the message.

Joseph's brothers bow respectfully, and keep their distance. Joseph then carries on a conversation with his brothers through the interpreter, his steward.

Joseph: Ask them, "Why have you come? You are not from my country."

Steward: *(to the brothers)* **His majesty asks, "Why have you come? You are not from his country."**

Reuben: Please tell him sir, that the famine is very severe in our country as well. We are from the land of Canaan. We heard that there is grain in Egypt, and we have come to purchase some for our families.

Steward: *(to Joseph quietly)* **And your answer?**

Joseph: Tell them that I said I am not fooled---I know they are spies who have come to secretly discover the weaknesses of our land.

Steward: *(to Joseph's brothers)* **His majesty does not believe you. He says he is not fooled by you---he knows you are spies, and that your purpose here is to discover the weaknesses of our land.**

Joseph's brothers are shocked and aghast at this turn of affairs, and protest their innocence.

Reuben: Sir, I beg you, please tell him that we are honest men. We are family---we are all the sons of one man, and we have come to buy food. We are not spies.

Steward:	*(quietly to Joseph)* **What shall I say?**
Joseph:	**I will pretend to be angry.** *(He slams his fist down in anger)* **Tell them I said they are spies indeed---I will not be deceived.**
Steward:	*(to Joseph's brothers)* **His majesty is not convinced. He says to tell you that you cannot deceive him---you are indeed spies.**
Simeon:	**Tell him everything. We have to make him believe us.**
Reuben:	**Everything?**
Simeon:	**Enough that he knows we are a family.**
Reuben:	*(to the steward)* **Sir, we are a family of twelve brothers, all from one man, who lives in the land of Canaan. The youngest of us is still with his father, and one is deceased.**
Steward:	*(to Joseph quietly)* **Did you hear that? Your father is alive! And so is your younger brother. But they think you are dead.**
Joseph:	**Yes, I heard.** *(he puts his head down for a moment to control his emotions)* **You must tell them that I will not relent--that I know they are spies. If they want to prove otherwise, they will be tested.**

(They both lower their voices to discuss this)

Steward:	**His majesty states that he still does not believe you. He insists you are spies. You will remain in his prison, until your younger brother comes here. One of you may return to your country to get your brother. That is the only way he will know if you are telling the truth.**

Guards come in and escort Joseph's brothers out of the room to the palace prison. (offstage)

Joseph:	*(to his steward)* **What do you think?**
Steward:	**Your majesty concealed his true feelings very well.**
Joseph:	**Do you perceive my true feelings? You can tell me this without fear.**

Steward:	I perceive that your Majesty loves his family very much despite what they did to you.
Joseph:	And you are right. This test is for me, also---I must keep myself free of any bitterness, or it will be a chain around my neck, dragging me down.

Asenath enters, and the steward bows politely and exits, to give them privacy to talk.

Joseph:	*(very lovingly)* **Asenath, come, I must speak with you.**
Asenath:	The house servants are saying that your brothers are here!
Joseph:	Yes, they have come. That is why I wanted to talk with you.
Asenath:	Where are they?
Joseph:	They are in the prison.
Asenath:	*(gasps)* **Do you seek revenge?**
Joseph:	No. And I want you and the others in our household to understand the meaning of my actions. My brothers do not know my identity yet; this must be kept secret. I am pretending to accuse them of being spies.
Asenath:	*(puzzled)* **Why?**
Joseph:	I am testing them---to see if they feel conviction and remorse for what they did. I need to know if they have changed.
Asenath:	And if they have not?
Joseph:	(sighs) I do not know what I will do then---I only hope I do not have to choose. But this plan will not work unless I can keep my identity hidden from them.
Asenath:	I will gather the household servants and explain the need for secrecy. *She turns to go, then turns back for a moment)* **Joseph---**

Joseph: Yes; what is it?

Asenath: I know that you love them and care about them. I understand your need to test them; but please do not torment yourself. You will torture yourself by leaving them in the prison for a long time.

Joseph: I love you, Asenath. You are a gift from God. Do not worry; I will release them in three days---all except one.

Asenath: Will the test be over then?

Joseph: No. That is only the beginning.

Joseph and Asenath exit together.

PART NINE: A FAMILY SECRET

NARRATOR: Joseph never lost his hope and trust in God, though he went through many painful situations. His character was shaped by these trials, and he became a person who was devoted to helping others. The 7 year famine, which was foretold in Pharaoh's dream, now became a reality. It was Joseph's job to oversee the dispersion of the grain which had been stored up for this national disaster. However, the famine spread beyond Egypt; all the surrounding countries were affected as well. And so it was that Joseph's own brothers came to Egypt to buy food. Joseph recognized them, but they did not know who he was. He decided to test them to see if they had changed, so he accused them of being spies, and held them in prison for 3 days. Joseph speaks to his brothers through an interpreter to disguise his identity, so his brothers are unaware that he understands their native language.

Have the platform with Joseph's throne on the stage.
Joseph's steward enters with Joseph's brothers.

Steward: There has been a change in plans. Wait here.   *(He exits briefly)*

Reuben: Those 3 days in prison seemed like 3 years. I am glad to be out of chains. *(He rubs his wrists)*

Simeon: Did he say plans have changed? Do you think he intends to execute us?

Reuben: If he does intend to, there is no escape. We are at his mercy.

Simeon: We must think of some reason it would be to his advantage to keep us alive.

Joseph enters and sits on his throne, accompanied by guards who stand around the platform. He speaks with his steward, who then approaches the brothers.

Steward: His majesty says, "Do what I say and you will live, for I fear God." In order to prove your honesty, he will keep one of your brothers here in prison, while the rest of you go back and bring food to your families. But you must bring your youngest brother to him so that he will know you are truthful. Then he will let you live."

(He walks back to Joseph)

Judah: We are doomed. This is happening because of what we did to Joseph.

Simeon: God is punishing us.

Judah: We had no mercy on the boy even when he was pleading for his life.

Reuben: I knew this would catch up with us one day. I warned you not to harm him! His blood is on our hands, and we are accountable. We may have deceived our father, but God is not fooled.

Joseph hears their words and turns away to hide his tears.

Steward: *(quietly to Joseph)* Your majesty, what should I do?

Joseph: *(he gains control over his emotions and turns around)* We will carry on with the plan. Guards! Arrest that man, *(he indicates Simeon)* bind him, and bring him to prison.

Two palace guards take Simeon, bind his hands, and march him away.

Simeon: *(as he is led away)* Brothers, take care of my family!

Joseph: *(quietly to his steward)* Accept their money, and fill their bags with grain, but secretly put each man's money back into his sack. Also, give them food for their journey home. I must seek privacy to pray.

(Joseph exits)

Joseph's steward and two guards remain with the brothers.

Reuben: *(to the steward)* **Sir, here is our money.** *(He offers him a money bag)* **We beg of you to allow us to purchase grain for our families.**

Steward: *(he accepts the money)* **His majesty is very compassionate; he will not let your families starve. Your donkeys have been taken care of in his majesty's stable while you were in prison, and your sacks of grain will be ready to load on your donkeys very soon. You may wait in the courtyard.**

Joseph's brothers all bow courteously and exit, and the steward exits.

During the following narration, put a screen in front of the platform with the throne.

(You will also need to put some kind of stool or chair by the screen — something that looks Arabic or like furniture that would be found in an ancient middle-eastern culture)

Narrator: Joseph's brothers were in for yet another unpleasant surprise, on their journey home. When they stopped for the night, they discovered that their money had been returned in the bags of grain. They realized with dismay that any attempt to appear honest was surely sabotaged now. They dreaded the moment when they would have to tell their father what had happened. And now that moment had come.

Jacob comes out to greet his sons as they arrive home.

Jacob: **Welcome home, my sons! I rejoice to see you safely home again!.....but, where is Simeon? What have you done with him?**

Reuben: **Father, he had to remain in Egypt.**

Jacob: **What? What is the meaning of this?**

Reuben: **Let me explain. The ruler of the land insisted that we were spies, and put us all in prison for 3 days.**

Jacob: Spies! Did you tell him you are my sons?

Judah: Yes, we did, but it didn't make any difference. He still accused us of lying.

Reuben: Father, here is the hardest part. When he found out that we have a younger brother at home, he said that we must prove our honesty by bringing this brother to him. He is keeping Simeon in prison there until we do this.

Jacob: Why did you tell him that you even have a younger brother! You will be the cause of my death! Joseph is dead, Simeon is gone, and now you would take Benjamin away from me? Never! Do you hear me? I said never! My son will not go back with you---he is all I have left of his mother!

Judah: Father, the man told us that we would never see his face again if we do not bring Benjamin back with us. Only then will he release Simeon.

Reuben: But there is something else we must tell you. This is the strangest part. On our way home, when we stopped for the night, we looked in the bags of grain, and all our money had been returned---it was in the sacks.

Jacob almost faints, and two of his sons catch him before he falls. They help him sit down.

Jacob: This is some kind of trick---to make you look like thieves! We are undone.

One of his sons brings him some water in a goblet, and helps him take a sip.
Then two of his sons help Jacob get up, and walk away. All exit.

Narrator: While Simeon was locked away in an Egyptian prison cell, his brothers and their father tried to make the grain last as long as possible. Jacob's sons were afraid that if they tried to take Benjamin with them, their father really would die from a heart attack. At last the inevitable day came when they had barely any food left.

Jacob and his sons come back to center stage.

Jacob: *(to his sons)* **You will have to go back to Egypt and buy food.**

Judah: **The man told us sternly that we could not go back without Benjamin. Father, I promise you that I will take care of Benjamin---I will do whatever is needed to keep him safe. And if I am not successful, I will bear the blame forever.**

Jacob: *(with a resigned air)* **If there is no way around this, then so be it.** *(sighs)* **But do this: bring gifts—honey, spices, almonds—the best we have. Placate the man, and perhaps he will treat you more kindly. Take back the money and more besides. May God grant you mercy in the sight of this man, so he will return your brothers to us. And may God give me strength to endure what happens.**

Jacob exits one direction as his sons exit in a different direction.

Narrator: And so the ten brothers packed their supplies, bid their father farewell, and departed on their journey back to the land of Egypt. They did not know what awaited them---whether it would be prison or death, or whether Simeon would still be alive. So many things still puzzled them; if the ruler thought they were spies, why had he sent them home with provisions for their journey? Why was there both harshness---and kindness? Perhaps they would find out soon.

PART TEN: REMEMBERING DREAMS

NARRATOR: The world-wide famine had been going on now for almost two years. God had warned Pharaoh in 2 dreams about the coming famine. There in Egypt God used a Hebrew slave named Joseph to explain the meaning of the dreams to Pharaoh, and to recommend a plan for survival. Pharaoh was so impressed with the wisdom that Joseph spoke, that he made Joseph second in command over the entire nation of Egypt, to take charge of storing up grain in preparation for this famine. Joseph now looked and spoke like an Egyptian, so his Hebrew brothers did not recognize him when they came to buy food in Egypt. Joseph knew who they were immediately, and he devised a plan to test their character and see if they had changed. It was his own brothers who had sold him into slavery. Joseph pretended to suspect his brothers of being spies, and held his brother Simeon in prison until they would return with their younger brother, in order to prove that they were telling the truth.

Have the small platform with Joseph's throne on it at center back stage. Joseph enters with Asenath. He sits on his throne, and she sits by his feet, or on a small stool close to his throne. (close enough to him that he can easily stroke her hair, which he does at first)

Asenath: Joseph…. Simeon has been in the prison for over a year. Do you think they have abandoned him? Do you think they will come after all?

Joseph: Their delay is a good sign---it means that my father may still be alive. He would be very reluctant to let Benjamin go. He was always very protective of Benjamin, because my mother died when Benjamin was born. He loved her so much, and Benjamin reminds him of her.

Asenath: Then why did you insist that they bring him?

Joseph: *(sighs)* It's part of the test to see if their character has changed. They were always so jealous of Benjamin and I because our mother was our father's favorite wife. They hated us---especially me.

Asenath: I'm so sorry.

Joseph: And I made it worse when I told them my dreams. I was so excited, that I didn't think. I should have kept it to myself. Of course, it antagonized them — in my dream, I was in a field, and my brothers' sheaves of wheat bowed down to my sheaf of wheat. In a second dream, I saw the sun, moon, and eleven stars bow down to me. My brothers thought I was so arrogant.

Asenath: But your dreams came true!

Joseph: Yes....when my brothers stood there before me bowing down, I remembered those dreams of long ago. How strange it all seems.

Joseph's steward comes in quickly — he is excited.

Steward: Your brothers have arrived, your majesty.

Joseph: *(he and Asenath stand)* **How many?**

Steward: There are ten.

Joseph: *(he lets out a sigh of relief)* **They have brought him! Take them to my house, and prepare a meal for them. They will eat with me at noon.**

(Joseph and Asenath exit)

Joseph's brothers enter along with several guards.
They stand at a little distance from the steward and are waiting for instructions.

Steward: You must come with me.

Reuben: Where? Where are you taking us?

Steward: His majesty's home.

Judah:	(to Reuben) He may intend to make us into slaves.

Reuben:	Sir, I can explain. We found our money in our sacks---we have brought it back to prove to you that we are not thieves. We don't know who put it there.

Steward:	Be at peace. Your grain was paid for. As for the money in your sacks, consider it a blessing from the Lord. Now come---you will be dining with his majesty at noon, and there are preparations to be made.

*Joseph's brothers give each other surprised perplexed looks, then they exit
with the steward during the following narration. (Also, during the narration,
you will need to put a screen in front of the throne as this next scene is in Joseph's home.)*

Narration: Now Joseph's brothers were more perplexed than ever. The behavior of this ruler was an enigma to them—a puzzle they could not figure out. And the steward spoke of the Lord as if he believed in Him, when everyone knew that Egyptians worshiped many idols, not the one true God. On their first visit to Egypt, they had been treated as spies, and now they were being treated as special guests. The steward even took care of their donkeys and supplies, and had water brought to wash their feet. And so they waited in the ruler's home for his arrival, with suspense rising in their hearts.

Joseph's brothers enter looking around at the interior of Joseph's home.

*Then the steward comes in escorting Simeon.
All the brothers are excited to see him and greet him.*

Reuben:	How are you, Simeon? Did they mistreat you?

Simeon:	No, I was well-cared for, even in prison---although I did have to do manual labor. But what took you so long?

Judah:	It's....complicated.

Reuben: You know Father---he would not consent to let Benjamin go, until the situation was desperate.

Simeon: Is my family well?

Reuben: They are, but we must return quickly with more food.

Joseph enters the room, and all his brothers bow down to him respectfully.

He stays at a distance from them, and his steward conveys his words to his brothers.

Joseph: *(to steward)* Ask them if their father is well.

Steward: His majesty wants to know if your father is well.

Reuben: Yes, please tell him that our father is alive and well.

Joseph: *(to steward)* Ask them to introduce their younger brother.

Steward: His majesty wishes you to introduce your youngest brother.

Judah: Your majesty, this is Benjamin, the one we told you about.

(*Benjamin steps up***)**

Steward: This is their youngest brother, Benjamin.

Joseph leaves the room quickly, to hide his tears.

Steward: *(to the brothers)* Please follow me---we will eat in this next room. His majesty will join you shortly.

The steward leads the way, and Joseph's brothers and the guards follow him offstage.

Narrator: Joseph's servants prepared a wonderful feast for his brothers. Joseph did not sit at their table, but his brothers were very astonished to see that Joseph had them seated at their own table according to their ages. They could not imagine how this ruler knew their ages. And after the feast, Joseph privately gave more instructions to his steward.

Joseph and his steward enter.

Joseph: Fill their bags with grain, and put their money back inside their bags on top of the grain. Do this for each one of them---but when you get to the bag of Benjamin, my youngest brother, put my silver cup in the top of the bag. Make sure that no one sees you doing this.

Steward: Yes, your majesty.

Joseph and his steward exit.

Narrator: Joseph's brothers prepared to leave the next morning. They felt secure and relieved and joyful. They were not kept hostage or as slaves, Simeon was released to them, and Benjamin was unharmed. And they had plenty of food to bring home to their families. What could possibly go wrong this time?

PART ELEVEN: THE SILVER CUP

NARRATOR: Joseph's brothers had finally come back to Egypt with their younger brother Benjamin. The strange and hostile ruler of Egypt had insisted that they would not be able to buy more food unless they brought this younger sibling. At last when they were in dire need of food because of the famine, their father finally consented and allowed Benjamin to go with his brothers. Their father Jacob feared he would lose this last son, as he had lost Joseph many years before. Now the brothers had completed their mission — they had purchased more food, and Benjamin was safe, and the ruler had finally released Simeon to come home. They felt secure and light-hearted; their dread and fears were over now. They began the trip home with a jovial manner, not knowing the trouble that loomed just ahead.

Joseph's brothers are walking across the stage, carrying bags on their shoulders.

(These drawstring bags can be made of canvas, muslin, or burlap and stuffed with a light material such as packing peanuts, shredded paper, etc.

Put a silver goblet in the bag Benjamin will carry)

Suddenly Joseph's steward appears and yells for them to stop.
He catches up with the brothers, followed by several of Joseph's guards.

Steward: **Stop! In the name of his Majesty, Zaphenath-Paneah of Egypt!**

Joseph's brothers comply, and are immediately surrounded by the guards.

Steward: **My master treated you kindly---he made a feast for you and gave you provisions for your journey home---and this is how you repay him? By stealing his silver cup---the very one he drinks from! How could you do such a wicked thing?**

Reuben: **Why does your master say such things? We would never do anything like that! We returned the money we found in the sacks, and extra besides, and we brought gifts to him.**

Judah: If the cup is found with any of us, that one will die, and the rest of us will be your master's slaves.

Steward: The one on whom it is found will be the slave; the rest of you may go free.

Judah: Go ahead; search our sacks. You won't find it.

Each brother lowers his bag, and the guards and steward begin searching each one. They come to Benjamin's bag last, and discover the silver goblet in it.

Steward: *(pointing to Benjamin)* **This is the thief! He must pay the penalty. I will take him back to my master.**

Two guards get on either side of Benjamin, and take him by the arms.

Reuben: **No! We will all go back.**

All of Joseph's brothers pick up their sacks and follow the steward and the guards, who are still treating Benjamin like their prisoner, and keeping him by them. They all exit, with the brothers walking in a manner that shows the dejection and dismay they are feeling.

During the following narration, bring out the platform and throne.

Narrator: Mere words cannot express the horror that Joseph's brothers felt when they saw that silver cup in Benjamin's sack. This was a garish nightmare, and how they wished they would wake up and discover that none of it was happening. But their dilemma was all too real. The guilt of their past deed weighed heavily on them, and kept them from having any confidence that God would answer them if they turned to Him for help. So they glumly marched on to meet their doom.

Joseph comes in and sits on his throne; his advisors stand around him. The steward and guards escort Joseph's brothers into the room.

Joseph: (to his steward) Tell them I said, "How could you do this to me? Don't you know that a man like me has supernatural knowledge?"

Steward: His Majesty wants to know how you could do this to him. He is a man who has supernatural knowledge, and you cannot hide things from him.

Judah: There is nothing we can say or do to prove our innocence in this matter. God has revealed our guilt. We must all become your slaves.

Steward: (to Joseph) What is your answer?

Joseph: Tell them I am just, and only the guilty one will remain as my slave.

Steward: His majesty will not allow that, for he is just. Only the guilty one will become a slave.

Judah: (he steps forward a little) Sir, we would not have brought our younger brother at all except that you required it. Years ago, his brother perished, and our father has been grieving ever since. Benjamin our brother is the only remaining child of his mother. If he does not return home, we fear our father will die of heartbreak. Your majesty, I beg of you, let me take his place, and send the young man home to his father. I cannot bear to see the misery that would come upon my father if he loses this son also. Let me stay and be your slave instead of him.

Joseph: (to his staff) Everyone, leave my presence.

All his staff quickly exits the room.

Joseph cannot contain his tears any longer, and begins to weep loudly. When he finally can speak, he motions to his brothers to come closer, and he steps down to meet them.

Joseph: I am Joseph, your brother. Is my father still alive?

The brothers are terrified and motionless with fear and look at one another in shock.

Joseph moves closer to them, but they are still paralyzed with fear.

Joseph: **I am your brother Joseph, the one you sold into slavery. You must forgive yourselves for what you did, for it was God who sent me here to save lives. God sent me on ahead of you to preserve your lives and the lives of many. We have five more years of famine ahead of us. You must go and bring back your entire families. I can take care of you here. Benjamin, tell Father about all you have seen here---tell him how I am a ruler over all of Egypt. Bring my father back here as soon as you can.**

Joseph embraces Benjamin, weeping with joy, and Benjamin weeps also.

Then Joseph hugs his brothers, and they exit together, rejoicing.

This dramatic encounter between the brothers should not be too brief;
Joseph should hug each of his brothers in turn. There should be great emotion
expressed---sorrow and joy mixed together as they see their long-lost brother.

The following narration can occur during this scene.

Narrator: This was the moment that Joseph had imagined so many times, and wondered if it ever could---or would---become a reality. And now that it was here, it still felt surreal, as if it were happening in a dream. Such intensity of emotion would be hard to describe---they didn't know whether to laugh or cry, so they did quite a bit of each. But there was a sense of something greater than human emotion---it was the supernatural peace of God, knowing that He had orchestrated all the events of their lives---even the evil ones---into something good----into this moment of restoration of a broken heart and a broken family.

PART TWELVE: FAMILY REUNION

NARRATOR: Joseph's dreams came true at last—all eleven of his brothers stood before him in the throne room of Egypt and bowed down to him because he was the ruler of Egypt. But that is not what gave him ultimate satisfaction---his greatest joy came when he could reveal who he was to his brothers, and they could be together again as a family. The sinful act that had separated them from each other was forgiven. Joseph urged them to bring their entire families to Egypt so that he could provide for them, for there were five more years of famine to endure.

Joseph and Asenath enter the throne room and sit down to talk.

Asenath: *(smiling happily)* **So your brothers passed your test.**

Joseph: **They acknowledged their guilt, and every one of them offered themselves as slaves. But when I said I would keep only Benjamin as a slave, it was Judah who begged to be allowed to take Benjamin's place.**

Asenath: **Do you think they understand why you gave them this test?**

Joseph: **I don't know---they are still in shock that I am even alive. And they are so ashamed of what they did when they sold me into slavery that it is hard for them to believe that I truly have forgiven them.**

Asenath: **Your love and faithfulness will prove it to them over time. I have never known a more loving and faithful person than you. It's what makes me love your God, for I know He put this inside you.**

Joseph: **He never left me---not even in the darkest times---when I was in the pit, or in the prison, I knew He was there with me. He is a faithful God. I know He loves me.**

Asenath: **The idols are not like that---we spent our lives in fear of them and trying to appease them. Now I know they are not gods at all.**

The steward enters and bows politely.

Steward: Your majesty, your brother has arrived and wishes to speak with you.

Asenath excuses herself, and exits. The steward ushers in Judah, then exits.

Joseph: Judah! *(he greets him with an embrace)* **How was your journey? How is father?**

Judah: *(smiling)* **Father had a very hard time believing our story that you are here, until he saw the wagons and food that Pharaoh sent for our journey.**

Joseph: I informed Pharaoh of your occupation as shepherds, and he has arranged for you to live in the province of Goshen, so that you will have plenty of grazing land for your livestock.

Judah: Thank you, my brother. *(he embraces him again)*

Joseph: I will have my guards escort you and your families there. Tell Father that I will soon be on my way there also, as soon as my chariot is ready.

Joseph and Judah exit together.

During the following narration, put a screen in front of the throne platform.

Narrator: As Joseph rode out to meet his father whom he had not seen in 22 years, he thought back over those years, and all the incredible things that God had done in that time. Who could have imagined that a slave boy would end up as a ruler in Egypt? It was impossible, yet it happened---because nothing is impossible with God. He is the one who created the world and the entire universe---out of nothing. Time and space are in His hands, and He orchestrates events to line up with His plans, and nothing can thwart His plans.

All of Joseph's brothers and his father are waiting on stage when Joseph enters.
Jacob moves to center and Joseph hurries to meet him. Joseph hugs his father and weeps.

Jacob: *(he pulls away to look at Joseph's face)* **Joseph, my son---it is really you! You have your mother's eyes......I thought I had lost you forever.** *(he hugs him again)* **God has brought you back to me.**

Joseph: **I must introduce you to Pharaoh---he is very glad you have come. I have brought extra chariots to take you to meet him. Reuben, Simeon, Levi, Judah, and Benjamin---please come with me now to speak with Pharaoh.**

Reuben: **What shall we say to him?**

Joseph: **When he asks about your occupation, explain that our family has always been shepherds for many generations. He may even want to hire some of you to help with his own livestock.**

The brothers and their father exit as they say these last lines.
Remove the screen during the narration to reveal the throne.

Narrator: Joseph felt like a young boy again, so excited was he to introduce his father, the patriarch of a great family, to the renowned king of Egypt. His brothers however were understandably uneasy at the prospect of meeting Pharaoh. They were already feeling the effects of coming to live in a strange culture. Joseph noticed this, and remembered how he felt when he was first brought to Egypt. He resolved in himself to help them make the adjustment.

Pharaoh enters the throne room and stands waiting. Joseph enters and bows courteously.

Joseph: **My father Jacob has arrived.**

Pharaoh: **Please bring him in. I have looked forward to meeting him.**

Joseph brings his father and brothers into the room, and escorts his father
closer to Pharaoh.

Joseph: This is my father.

Pharaoh: How was your journey?

Jacob: It went well, and I thank you for the wagons and provisions that you sent.

Pharaoh: Welcome to Egypt. Joseph tells me that you and your family are shepherds.

Jacob: For many generations, this has been our occupation.

Pharaoh: Then the land of Goshen will be yours, for your family and all your livestock.

Jacob: May the Lord bless you and make His face shine upon you.

Pharaoh: And these are your brothers?

Joseph: These are my older brothers: Reuben, Simeon, Levi, and Judah; and my younger brother, Benjamin. The others remained with the flocks.

Pharaoh: I am very pleased that you have come. And now if you will excuse me, I will not interrupt your family reunion. *(he exits)*

Joseph: There is someone else I would like you to meet. *(he beckons to someone unseen)*

Asenath enters with Ephraim and Manasseh

Joseph: This is my wife, Asenath. *(he takes her hand and escorts her to his father)*

Jacob: She is very beautiful. *(he pats her hand)* **And who are these?**

Joseph: These are the sons God has given me---Ephraim and Manasseh.

Joseph brings them closer to his father, who hugs them.

Jacob: I thought that I would never see your face again, and now God has allowed me to see your children. The Lord bless you, my sons.

Asenath: We have refreshments ready for you in the dining room. Would you join me?

Joseph's brothers follow her and her sons out.
Ephraim and Manasseh are already interacting with Benjamin on the way out.

Joseph: Asenath, we will come in just a moment.

Joseph and Jacob stay center stage.

Joseph: I know this change will not be easy for my brothers.

Jacob: Joseph, I am old. I don't know how long I have yet to live. I could die tomorrow.

Joseph: *(hugs Jacob tightly)* Don't say that! I finally have you here with me.

Jacob: Joseph, your brothers are afraid that after I die, you will take your revenge for all the wrong they did to you.

Joseph: Reuben, Simeon, Levi, and Judah---I need to speak with you.

The four brothers come back into the room with Joseph and Jacob.

Joseph: I want you to know that I did not bring you here so I could treat you badly and take revenge. You do not need to make it up to me by being my slaves. I have forgiven you. What happened was evil, but God has turned it into good for many people---many lives were saved. You do not need to blame yourself anymore, and I do not hold it against you any longer. You are forgiven.

Each of these brothers embraces Joseph, and they are all weeping then smiling.

Narrator: God does give dreams, and then He brings them to pass. God's dreams are always bigger than ours. Abraham asked only for one son, and God gave him as many descendants as the stars. And God's dreams always involve people---the lives He wants to save, and the lives He wants to bless….for eternity.

www.ingramcontent.com/pod-product-compliance
Lightning Source LLC
Chambersburg PA
CBHW081158090426
42736CB00017B/3373